tapas

tapas

RYLAND
PETERS
& SMALL
LONDON NEW YORK

First published in the USA in 2007
by Ryland Peters & Small, Inc.
519 Broadway, 5th Floor
New York NY 10012
www.rylandpeters.com

10 9 8 7 6 5 4

ISBN-10: 1-84597-395-X
ISBN-13: 978-1-84597-395-7

Printed and bound in China

Designer Jo Fernandes
Editor Rachel Lawrence
Picture Research Emily Westlake
Production Sheila Smith
Art Director Anne-Marie Bulat
Publishing Director Alison Starling

Notes

All spoon measurements are level unless
otherwise stated.
Grills, ovens, and broilers should be heated
to the required temperature before adding the food.
Eggs are large unless otherwise specified. Uncooked
or partially cooked eggs should not be served to the
very old, frail, young children, pregnant women, or
those with compromised immune systems.
Specialist Spanish ingredients are available in gourmet
stores, Spanish and sometimes Italian deli counters.

Library of Congress Cataloging-in-Publication Data
Beresford, Julz.
    Tapas / Julz Beresford, Clare Ferguson, and Linda Tubby.
        p. cm.
    Includes index.
    ISBN-13: 978-1-84597-395-7
    1. Appetizers--Spain. 2. Spanish cookery.
I. Ferguson, Clare. II. Tubby, Linda. III. Title.
    TX740.B4685 2007
    641.8'120946--dc22

                                2006028294

contents

a taste sensation

One of the defining features of Spanish food culture, tapas bars, or *tascas*, are found all over Spain. Before lunch or dinner, they are crowded with people catching up over a glass of sherry, wine, or beer accompanied by little savory snacks. From little bowls of marinated olives or chunks of Manchego cheese to deep-fried seafood, these delicious dishes are the ultimate in bar food.

The word *tapa* means lid and, while the subject of much debate, it is thought that this originally referred to a piece of bread placed on top of a glass of sherry to keep flies away. This was often served with a slice of cheese or ham and so the tradition began. Today the range of tapas dishes is astounding and reflects the diversity of ingredients in Spain, which include exquisite cured meats, seafood, and cheese, as well as delicate flavorings such as oak-smoked paprika and saffron.

While tapas is traditionally a pre-lunch or pre-dinner snack, it can be a meal in itself. The tapas crawl, or *tapeo*, is a long-standing tradition in many towns and cities, with customers moving from one bar to the next and sampling each one's specialties as they go.

Tapas is a wonderfully sociable way to eat and re-creating these irresistible dishes at home is a lot of fun. Many of them can be prepared in advance and served at a leisurely pace over several hours. So why not invite a few friends around, crack open a bottle of Rioja, and feast upon this sensational fingerfood.

fish and shellfish

albóndigas de bacalao
cod balls

Put the cod in a bowl, cover with cold water, and keep in the refrigerator for at least 24 hours. Change the water occasionally.

Prick the potatoes with a skewer, then bake in a preheated oven at 400°F for 1 hour or until soft on the inside. Scoop the flesh out of the skins into a bowl and mash.

Put the cod in a saucepan, cover with cold water, add the bay leaf, bring to a boil, and simmer for 30 minutes. Let cool, then remove the skin and flake the flesh into a bowl, making sure to remove all the bones. Add to the mashed potatoes, then stir in the garlic, parsley, pepper, and 2 tablespoons of the cod cooking liquid. Roll the mixture into small balls. Put in a bowl, cover with plastic wrap, and chill in the refrigerator for 2–3 hours.

Put the egg in a bowl, add 1 tablespoon water, and beat lightly. Dip the cod balls in the egg, then roll in flour on a plate. Fill a deep skillet or an electric deep-fryer one-third with oil, or to the manufacturer's recommended level. Heat to 380°F or until a ½-inch cube of bread browns in 30 seconds. Cook the balls, in batches, for about 3 minutes or until golden brown. Remove with a slotted spoon and drain on crumpled paper towels. Serve hot with alioli.

4 oz. salt cod

10 oz. potatoes

1 bay leaf

1 garlic clove, crushed

1 tablespoon freshly chopped flat-leaf parsley

freshly ground white pepper

1 egg

all-purpose flour

oil, for frying

alioli (page 58) or lemon wedges, to serve

an electric deep-fryer (optional)

serves 4

gambas al ajillo
garlic shrimp

48 small uncooked shrimp,
about 1¼ lb., shelled and
deveined, with tail shell
left on

4 tablespoons extra virgin
olive oil

8 garlic cloves, bruised

6 small dried chiles

8 small fresh bay leaves

juice of ½ lemon

sea salt

alioli (page 58), to serve

4 individual cazuelas
(terra cotta ramekins)
preheated in a hot oven

serves 4

To prepare the shrimp, put them on a plate and sprinkle lightly
with salt. Heat the olive oil in a skillet, add the garlic and fry until
brown. Add the chiles, bay leaves, and shrimp all at once and fry
without turning until the shrimp are crusted and curled on one
side, then turn them over and crust the other side, about 3½
minutes in total.

Transfer to the preheated cazuelas, sprinkle with lemon juice,
and top with a spoonful of alioli, or serve a small bowl of alioli
on the side. Serve immediately while still bubbling hot.

boquerones en vinagre
marinated anchovies

To clean the anchovies, run your finger down the belly side and open up the fish. Pull the spine from the head and separate it from the flesh. Remove the head. Wash the fish and let dry on paper towels.

Put the anchovies in a plastic container and pour in the vinegar. Let marinate in the refrigerator overnight. Rinse the anchovies and put in a serving dish with the garlic, parsley, and olive oil. Cover and chill overnight in the refrigerator. Return to room temperature before serving with bread or as an accompaniment to another dish. You can return them to the refrigerator to eat another day—they only get better with time.

*Note If fresh anchovies are unavailable, use any small fish, such as smelts or tiny sardines. Aim for 2–3 inches long.

6 oz. fresh anchovies*

scant ½ cup good-quality white vinegar

3 garlic cloves, sliced

1 tablespoon chopped fresh flat-leaf parsley

scant ½ cup olive oil

serves 4

tigre tapas
mussels in overcoats

Tap the mussels gently against the work surface and discard any that don't close. Put the mussels, onion, bay leaves, and stock in a large saucepan and cover. Bring to a boil and cook hard for 2–3 minutes or until the shells open, then remove the cooked mussels and discard any that haven't opened. Boil the cooking liquid for several minutes to intensify the flavor, then pour through a strainer. Reserve ½ cup of the cooking liquid.

Fill a deep skillet or an electric deep-fryer one-third full with oil, or to the manufacturer's recommended level. Heat to 375°F or until a ½-inch cube of bread browns in 30 seconds.

To make the batter, sift the flour, paprika, and black pepper into a bowl. Grind the saffron threads finely with the salt using a mortar and pestle. Add to the dry ingredients. Put the egg whites in another bowl and beat until soft peaks form, then set aside.

Add the reserved mussel liquid and egg yolks to the flour and beat to make a soft batter. Fold in the egg whites.

Dip the mussels, still on their half-shells, into the batter. Add to the hot oil, in batches of 5–6. Cook for 2–2½ minutes or until golden, crisp, and fragrant, then serve.

1 lb. large, live mussels, in the shell, scrubbed, rinsed, and debearded

1 onion, sliced

2 fresh bay leaves, bruised

⅔ cup hot stock, white wine, or fino sherry

extra virgin olive oil or peanut oil, for deep-frying

batter

⅔ cup all-purpose flour

1 teaspoon oak-smoked hot Spanish paprika (page 23)

½ teaspoon freshly ground black pepper

a pinch of saffron threads

½ teaspoon coarse sea salt

2 eggs, separated

an electric deep-fryer (optional)

serves 4

almejas a la marinera

clams in tomato and saffron sauce

1 lb. small fresh clams

a pinch of saffron threads

1 tablespoon olive oil

½ small onion, finely chopped

2 garlic cloves, crushed

½ cup dry sherry

2 tablespoons tomato paste

1 tablespoon freshly chopped flat-leaf parsley

a pinch of oak-smoked sweet Spanish paprika (page 23)

a pinch of cayenne

1 tablespoon ground almonds

bread, to serve

serves 4

To clean the clams, put them in a bowl of cold salty water and let soak for 2 hours. This should help get rid of some of the grit. Put the saffron threads in a bowl with 1 tablespoon of hot water and let soak.

Heat the olive oil in a casserole dish over gentle heat, then add the onion and cook for 3 minutes. Add the garlic, sherry, tomato paste, parsley, paprika, cayenne, saffron with its juice, and ¼ cup water. Bring to a boil and boil for 4 minutes.

Add the clams, cover with a lid, and cook for 4 minutes until the shells steam open (discard any that don't). Stir in the ground almonds and cook for 1 further minute. Remove from the heat and set aside, covered with a lid, for 5 minutes. Serve warm with plenty of bread to mop up the juices.

sepia con alioli
squid with mayonnaise

⅔–1⅓ cups semolina flour

½–1 teaspoon sea salt

½–1 teaspoon dried oregano or marjoram leaves, crumbled

8 medium squid or cuttlefish tubes, sliced into ½-inch rounds

extra virgin olive oil, for deep-frying

alioli, to serve (page 58)

lemon halves, to serve

an electric deep-fryer (optional)

serves 4

Put the semolina flour, salt, and oregano in a bowl. Pat the squid or cuttlefish rings dry with paper towels and toss them in the flour mixture until well coated.

Fill a deep skillet or an electric deep-fryer one-third full with oil, or to the manufacturer's recommended level. Heat to 375°F or until a ½-inch cube of bread browns in 30 seconds. Fry the prepared squid or cuttlefish in the hot oil in batches of about 8. Cook for 30–45 seconds, the minimum time it takes to set the seafood to firm whiteness and make the coating crisp. Remove, drain, and keep hot. Continue until all are cooked.

Serve a pile of squid rings on each plate, with ½ lemon, if using, and a large spoonful of alioli.

pulpo a la vinagreta
marinated octopus

Bring a large saucepan of water to a boil, then blanch the octopus for 30 seconds at a time, repeating 4–5 times. Return to the saucepan, cover with a lid, and simmer for 1 hour.

Test the octopus for tenderness—if it's still tough, continue cooking for another 20 minutes. Remove from the heat, let cool, then drain. Cut the tentacles into 1-inch lengths and the bodies into bite-size pieces.

Heat the olive oil in a skillet, then add the vinegar, garlic, 2 tablespoons of the parsley, paprika, pepper flakes, capers, and octopus. Bring to a boil, then simmer for 3 minutes. Transfer to a plastic or ceramic dish, let cool, season, then let marinate in the refrigerator overnight.

Serve at room temperature with lemon juice and parsley.

about 12 oz. small octopus tentacles

3 tablespoons fruity olive oil

2 tablespoons red wine vinegar

2 garlic cloves, crushed

3 tablespoons freshly chopped flat-leaf parsley, plus extra to serve

½ teaspoon oak-smoked sweet Spanish paprika (page 23)

½ teaspoon dried hot red pepper flakes

1 tablespoon capers, chopped

juice of 1 lemon

sea salt and freshly ground black pepper

serves 4

meat and poultry

cordero al limón
lamb with lemon

Cut the lamb into ¾-inch cubes, put in a bowl, cover with the pineapple slices, and let marinate overnight, covered, in the refrigerator.

Stick the cloves into the lemon half and put it in a roasting dish. Add the garlic, olive oil, and rosemary. Remove the lamb from the pineapple and rub in the onion and paprika. Add the lamb to the roasting dish and cook in a preheated oven at 300°F for 15 minutes. Remove the dish from the oven, cover with aluminum foil and set aside for 10 minutes. Serve warm.

*Note Spanish paprika is available in three forms: *pimentón dulce* is mild and sweet; *pimentón picante* is spicy hot; while *pimentón agridulce* is bittersweet. There are also smoked versions which are made from chiles hung whole in traditional mud houses above oak fires that burn for 10–15 days. All these varieties are available in large supermarkets or specialty food shops.

8 oz. lean lamb

8 oz. canned
pineapple slices

10 cloves

1 lemon, halved

5 garlic cloves

2 tablespoons olive oil

a sprig of rosemary

½ small onion,
finely chopped

a pinch of oak-smoked
sweet Spanish paprika*

serves 4

pinchitos morunos
spicy moorish kabobs

2 tablespoons olive oil

2 garlic cloves, crushed

1 dried red chile, crushed

1 teaspoon ground cumin

1 teaspoon ground fennel

1 teaspoon oak-smoked sweet Spanish paprika (page 23)

juice of 1 lemon

2 tablespoons freshly chopped flat-leaf parsley

1 tablespoon dry sherry

1 lb. lean pork fillet

metal kabob skewers, or bamboo, soaked in water for 30 minutes

serves 4

Put the oil, garlic, chile, cumin, fennel, paprika, lemon juice, parsley, and sherry in a bowl and mix well. Cut the pork into ¾-inch cubes and add to the bowl. Cover and chill overnight in the refrigerator.

When ready to cook, preheat a broiler until very hot. Thread the pork onto the skewers and broil for 10 minutes, turning often—take care not to overcook the meat. Remove from the heat and set aside for 10 minutes. Serve warm.

6 oz. minced pork

6 oz. minced veal

1 teaspoon lemon juice

1 small onion, chopped

4 garlic cloves, crushed

2 tablespoons freshly chopped flat-leaf parsley

½ teaspoon grated nutmeg

½ teaspoon ground cloves

¼ cup dried bread crumbs

1 egg

1 tablespoon light cream

2 tablespoons olive oil

½ cup white wine

14 oz. canned tomatoes

½ teaspoon oak-smoked sweet Spanish paprika (page 23)

1 fresh bay leaf

sea salt and freshly ground white pepper

all-purpose flour, for dusting

serves 4

albóndigas
meat balls in tomato sauce

To make the meat balls, put the pork and veal in a bowl, then add the lemon juice, half of the chopped onion and crushed garlic, followed by the parsley, nutmeg, cloves, bread crumbs, egg, cream, salt, and pepper. Mix well, then roll into small balls. Dust with flour.

Heat the olive oil in a casserole dish until smoking, then add the meat balls, and fry until browned on all sides. Reduce the heat to low. Add the wine, chopped tomatoes, the remaining onion and garlic, with the paprika, bay leaf, and ⅓ cup water. Cover and simmer for 1 hour. The mixture should be quite liquid, so add extra water if necessary. Serve warm.

Note These meat balls can be made in advance as they will reheat well.

chorizo al vino
chorizo in red wine

Cut the chorizo into ½-inch cubes. Heat half the olive oil in a large, nonstick skillet until very hot. Add half the chorizo and fry on both sides for 1 minute each. Remove with a slotted spoon and keep hot. Add the remaining oil and remaining chorizo. Cook and remove as before.

Add the wine and thyme, if using, to the pan and swirl to dissolve the sediment. Cook gently to thicken and reduce the sauce. Pour the sauce over the hot chorizo, sprinkle with pepper and serve with chunks of torn bread for dipping.

Note Chorizo comes in many different varieties—you can get smoked, unsmoked, fresh, and cured. A spicy chorizo works well in this recipe. If chorizo is difficult to find, use cooked, garlicky Polish pork sausage (kielbasa) and add 2 teaspoons of paprika to the juices in the pan.

1½ lb. uncooked chorizo or other dense, garlic-flavored pork sausage

2 tablespoons extra virgin olive oil

⅔ cup red wine

4 sprigs of thyme (optional)

freshly ground black pepper

torn bread, for dipping

serves 4

ensalada catalana de garbanzos
catalan chickpea salad

Heat the olive oil in a skillet, add the onion, garlic, chorizo, and bay leaves and sauté over gentle heat for 5 minutes or until softened but not browned. Stir in the pine nuts and chickpeas with a little of their liquid. Heat through until the flavors are combined, mashing a little with a fork.

Sprinkle with pepper and chopped tomato and serve hot, warm or cool, but never chilled.

Note This recipe uses chorizo or sausage for ease, although traditionally it would have been made with pieces of chopped cooked pork, or sometimes *morcilla* (black pudding) or *butifarra* (white sausage).

3 tablespoons extra virgin olive oil

1 red onion, sliced

2 garlic cloves, chopped

8 oz. chorizo or other dense garlic-flavored pork sausage, sliced

2 bay leaves, bruised

2 tablespoons pine nuts, toasted in a dry skillet

2 cups canned chickpeas, drained, with 2 tablespoons of their liquid

coarsely ground black pepper

1 small tomato, finely chopped

serves 4

1 cup milk

½ small onion, sliced

1 bay leaf

2 peppercorns

a sprig of thyme

2 tablespoons unsalted butter

3 tablespoons all-purpose flour

a pinch of oak-smoked sweet Spanish paprika (page 23)

a pinch of freshly grated nutmeg

6 oz. jamón serrano (Spanish ham), finely chopped

4 oz. cooked chicken breast, finely chopped

2 cups dried bread crumbs

2 eggs, lightly beaten

oil, for deep-frying

an electric deep-fryer (optional)

serves 4

croquetas de jamón
ham croquettes

Put the milk in a saucepan, add the onion, bay leaf, peppercorns, and thyme and heat until just below boiling point. Remove from the heat, let cool, then strain into a bowl.

Put the butter in the saucepan, melt gently, stir in the flour, and cook for 2 minutes, stirring constantly. When the roux begins to brown, slowly add the strained milk, stirring to prevent lumps forming. Continue to cook, stirring in the paprika and nutmeg.

Heat 1 tablespoon oil in a skillet, add the ham and fry until the fat starts to run. Add the ham and chicken to the white sauce and cook until the sauce thickens, about 2 minutes. Remove from the heat and let cool. Refrigerate for 3 hours or overnight.

Shape the mixture into croquettes about 1 x 2 inches. Lightly roll in the bread crumbs, dip in the beaten eggs, and roll in the bread crumbs again. Chill for 1 hour or overnight.

When ready to cook, fill a saucepan or deep-fryer one-third with oil, or to the manufacturer's recommended level. Heat to 380°F or until a ½-inch cube of bread browns in 30 seconds. Fry the croquettes, in batches if necessary, for 3 minutes or until golden brown. Serve immediately.

pollo al ajillo
chicken with garlic

1 tablespoon sweet
Spanish paprika (page 23)

1 tablespoon
all-purpose flour

3½ lb. chicken pieces,
such as thighs and breasts
(but no drumsticks)

½ cup extra virgin olive oil

15 garlic cloves, unpeeled
but slightly bruised

1 fresh bay leaf

½ cup medium dry sherry

1 tablespoon coarsely
chopped fresh flat-leaf
parsley, plus extra to serve

sea salt and freshly ground
black pepper

a heat-diffusing mat

serves 4

Put the paprika, flour, salt, and pepper in a plastic bag and shake
to mix. Add the chicken pieces and toss again until the chicken is
evenly coated. Leave in the bag for 30 minutes or longer.

Heat the olive oil in a skillet, add the garlic, and fry for 2 minutes,
then remove with a slotted spoon. Add the chicken pieces (if
necessary do half at a time, but remember to remove half the
garlic-infused oil) and fry for 5 minutes. Add the fried garlic and
continue cooking for 5 minutes until the chicken is golden on
all sides.

Add the bay leaf and sherry and bring to a boil. Lower the heat
and simmer gently on a heat-diffusing mat for about 30 minutes
until tender. (Breast pieces will cook faster, so remove them
about 10 minutes before the end of cooking.) Pile onto a serving
platter and sprinkle with parsley.

Note Although Pollo al Ajillo is traditionally cooked on top of
the stove, it could be baked in a preheated oven at 375°F for
35 minutes or until cooked through.

vegetables and
little extras

gazpacho

Grind the garlic with a pinch of salt using a mortar and pestle.

Put the bread in a saucer with a little water and let soak. Put the ground garlic, bread, tomatoes, onion, cucumber, and vinegar in a blender and purée until smooth. Keep the motor running and add the olive oil in a slow and steady stream. Add salt and pepper to taste, then add the sugar.

Pour the mixture through a strainer into a bowl, adding more salt, pepper, and vinegar if necessary. Chill in the refrigerator overnight and serve in small bowls or glasses with a little chopped cucumber on top.

1 garlic clove

1 slice white bread, crusts removed

4 ripe juicy tomatoes, skinned and seeded

1 tablespoon grated onion

¼ small cucumber, peeled and seeded, plus extra to serve

1 tablespoon Spanish red wine vinegar

2 tablespoons olive oil

1 teaspoon sugar

sea salt and freshly ground black pepper

serves 4

tortilla española
spanish omelet

1 cup olive oil

4 potatoes, about 1 lb.,
cut into ½-inch cubes

1 onion, thinly sliced

6 eggs

4 tablespoons chopped
flat-leaf parsley (optional)

coarse sea salt and freshly
ground black pepper

a deep skillet,
9 inches diameter

serves 4

Heat the olive oil in a skillet until hot, add the potatoes and
onions, turn to coat with the oil, then reduce the temperature.
Cook for 15 minutes or until soft, turning often without letting
them brown. Remove the potatoes and onions with a slotted
spoon and drain on paper towels. Pour the oil into a small bowl.

Put the eggs, salt, and pepper into a bowl and beat with a fork.
Add the potatoes and onions to the bowl, stir gently, then stir in
the parsley, if using. Set aside for 10 minutes.

Put 2 tablespoons of the reserved oil in the skillet and heat until
smoking. Pour in the potato and egg mixture, spreading the
potatoes evenly in the pan. Cook for 1 minute, then reduce the
heat to medium and shake the pan often to stop it sticking.
When the eggs are brown underneath and top nearly firm, put
a large plate on the top and flip the omelet onto the plate. Add
4 tablespoons of the remaining oil to the pan and slide the
omelet back into the pan to brown the other side. Lower the heat
and flip the omelet 3 more times, cooking 1 minute each side, to
give it a good shape. It should remain juicy inside.

Transfer to a plate, brush the top with oil, and let stand until cool.
Serve in squares or wedges.

patatas bravas
potatoes in tomato sauce

3 tablespoons olive oil

1¼ lb. potatoes, cut into ¾-inch cubes

1 small onion, grated

3 garlic cloves, crushed

2 tablespoons fino sherry

4 oz. canned chopped tomatoes

½ teaspoon hot red pepper flakes, well crushed

½ teaspoon grated orange zest

1 teaspoon sugar

1 tablespoon freshly chopped flat-leaf parsley

1 fresh bay leaf

serves 4

Heat 2 tablespoons of the olive oil in a skillet, add the potatoes, and mix well. Cook for 15 minutes until golden brown.

Meanwhile, heat the remaining oil in another skillet, add the onion, and cook gently for 5 minutes. Add the garlic and sherry, then simmer for 1 minute to burn off the alcohol. Reduce the heat and add the tomatoes, pepper flakes, orange zest, sugar, parsley, and bay leaf. Cook for 10 minutes, adding a little water to stop the mixture thickening too much.

Transfer the cooked potatoes to a serving bowl, pour over the tomato sauce, and mix well. This can be made a day in advance and reheated before serving.

champiñones rellenos
stuffed mushrooms

Clean the mushrooms and remove the stems. Finely chop 2 of the stems and put them in a bowl. Add the milk and bread crumbs and let soak for 10 minutes.

Add the onion, garlic, parsley, ground pork, and ham. Mix together well, then cover with plastic wrap and let marinate in the refrigerator overnight.

When ready to cook, put 1 heaped teaspoon of the mixture in each of the mushroom caps. Swirl over a little olive oil, then cook in a preheated oven at 350°F for 15 minutes.

Remove from the oven, add a little pimiento to each one, and sprinkle with lemon juice. Serve warm.

8 medium mushrooms

2 tablespoons milk

2 tablespoons bread crumbs

2 tablespoons finely chopped onion

1 garlic clove, crushed

1 tablespoon freshly chopped flat-leaf parsley

2 tablespoons ground pork

1 tablespoon finely chopped jamón serrano (Spanish ham)

1 tablespoon canned chopped pimiento

1 tablespoon freshly squeezed lemon juice

olive oil, for drizzling

serves 4

piquillos rellenos
spanish stuffed peppers

Drain the piquillo peppers, reserving the liquid. Pat dry with paper towels.

Heat the olive oil, garlic, and part-drained white beans in a nonstick skillet and mash with a fork to a thick, coarse paste. Add 1 tablespoon of the sherry vinegar and 1 tablespoon of bean liquid, stir, then season well with salt and pepper. Let cool slightly, then stuff each piquillo with the mixture and sprinkle with the thyme.

Cut each piquillo pepper into thick slices or leave whole. Serve on 4 plates, adding some salad greens to each. Trickle over a tablespoon of the bean liquid and a few drops of vinegar, if using, before serving.

Variation Instead of canned piquillos or pimientos, use 4 sweet red peppers, halved lengthwise and seeded. Broil them skin side up until blistered and black. Transfer to a plastic bag, seal, and let steam. Rub off the skins, stuff with the mixture, roll up, then serve as in the main recipe.

6 oz. canned peeled piquillo peppers or pimientos

4 tablespoons olive oil

3–4 garlic cloves, chopped

2 cups canned white beans, such as cannellini or lima beans, part-drained, liquid reserved

2 tablespoons sherry vinegar (optional)

a handful of fresh thyme or mint, chopped

a handful of baby salad greens such as spinach, watercress, or flat-leaf parsley

sea salt and freshly ground black pepper

serves 4

1 large eggplant,
about 12 oz.

6–7 oz. strong, meltable
cheese such as Cabrales
or Cheddar

⅔ cup all-purpose flour,
seasoned with sea salt
and black pepper

2 eggs, well beaten

2 cups olive, sunflower, or
grapeseed oil, for frying

salsa

2 medium vine-ripened
tomatoes, chopped

¼ cup chile oil or olive oil
mixed with ½ teaspoon
Tabasco sauce

4 teaspoons red wine
vinegar or sherry vinegar

12 fresh basil leaves

sea salt and freshly ground
black pepper

toothpicks

an electric deep-fryer
(optional)

serves 4

berenjenas con queso
eggplant cheese fritters

Using a sharp, serrated knife, cut the eggplant crosswise into
18–24 thin slices about ¼ inch thick. Slice the cheese into pieces
of the same thickness. Cut and piece them together to fit,
sandwiching a piece of cheese between 2 pieces of eggplant.
To keep the "sandwiches" closed during cooking, push a
toothpick, at an angle, through each one.

Put the seasoned flour on a plate. Pour the beaten egg into a
shallow dish. Dip the eggplant "sandwiches" first into the flour,
then into the egg, then in flour again to coat well all over.

Fill a deep skillet or an electric deep-fryer one-third full with the
oil, or to the manufacturer's recommended level. Heat to 375°F
or until a ½-inch cube of bread browns in 30 seconds. Slide some
of the prepared "sandwiches" into the hot oil in batches of 3 and
fry for 2–3 minutes on the first side. Using tongs, turn and cook
for 1–2 minutes on the other side or until golden and crispy, with
the cheese melting inside. Drain on crumpled paper towels while
you coat and cook the rest.

To make the salsa, put the tomatoes, chile oil, vinegar, basil, salt,
and pepper in a food processor. Pulse in brief bursts to a coarse
mixture, then serve with the fritters.

pisto manchego
zucchini, tomato, and pepper stew

2 tablespoons olive oil

2 oz. jamón serrano (Spanish ham), prosciutto, or Smithfield, finely chopped

½ onion, finely chopped

4 garlic cloves, crushed

1 zucchini, chopped

2 tomatoes, skinned, seeded, and chopped

½ red bell pepper, seeded and chopped

1 tablespoon chopped fresh oregano leaves

a pinch of oak-smoked sweet Spanish paprika (page 23)

sea salt and freshly ground white pepper

serves 4

Heat the olive oil in a skillet, add the ham and onion, and cook over low heat for 5 minutes. Add the garlic, zucchini, tomatoes, bell pepper, oregano, and paprika. Simmer over low heat for 15 minutes, then add salt and pepper to taste, and serve.

Note This is a popular vegetable dish from central Spain, where there are two versions—one with meat and one without. Simply leave the jamón serrano out for a vegetarian dish. Both versions can be made a day in advance and reheat well.

pimientos picantes
marinated bell peppers

Broil the peppers slowly until the skins are blistered and black. Transfer to a plastic bag, seal, and let steam. When cool, pull off the skins and remove the seeds and membranes. Put the peppers in a strainer set over a bowl to catch the juices, then cut into ½-inch strips.

Heat a heavy-based skillet, then add the olive oil, vinegar, thyme, rosemary, garlic, cayenne, and the pepper juices. Cook over low heat for 2 minutes. Add the peppers, capers, parsley, and salt and pepper to taste. Cook, stirring, for 1 minute. Remove from the heat and let cool. Cover and chill overnight.

To serve, return to room temperature and serve on a thin slice of bread. This dish can be kept in the refrigerator for up to a week.

3 small red bell peppers

3 tablespoons olive oil

¼ cup sherry vinegar

a sprig of thyme

a sprig of rosemary

2 garlic cloves, sliced

½ teaspoon cayenne

1 tablespoon salted capers, rinsed and drained

1 tablespoon freshly chopped flat-leaf parsley

sea salt and freshly ground white pepper

thinly sliced bread, to serve

serves 4

espinacas con piñones y pasas
spinach, pine nuts, and raisins

Soak the raisins in warm water for 3 minutes, then drain.

Heat the olive oil in a skillet, add the pine nuts and garlic, cook for 1 minute, then add the sherry and boil for 1 minute.

Add the spinach and paprika and toss well to coat with the juices. Cook over low heat for 5 minutes. Add the drained raisins and season with salt and pepper to taste, then serve.

½ cup raisins

2 tablespoons fruity olive oil

½ cup pine nuts, toasted in a dry skillet

2 garlic cloves, sliced

3 tablespoons dry sherry

8 oz. spinach, about 2 cups

a pinch of oak-smoked sweet Spanish paprika (page 23)

sea salt and freshly ground black pepper

serves 4

pinchos

2 tablespoons olive oil

1 garlic clove, crushed

½ teaspoon hot red pepper flakes

leaves from 2 sprigs of thyme, plus extra to serve

4 oz. white asparagus, in can or jar*

2 tablespoons slivered almonds, ground to a paste with a mortar and pestle

½ canned pimiento, chopped

8 slices of white bread, lightly toasted

sea salt and freshly ground black pepper

serves 4

Put the olive oil, garlic, pepper flakes, and thyme in a saucepan, bring to a boil, then remove from the heat. Let cool.

Put the asparagus in a blender and pulse until smooth. Slowly add the strained oil and blend again. Mix in the ground almonds and salt and pepper to taste.

Slice the pimiento into thin strips. Spoon the asparagus mixture onto the toasted bread and top with the sliced pimiento. Add a few thyme leaves and serve on a tray for your guests to help themselves.

*Note White asparagus, sold in cans or jars, is a traditional Spanish ingredient.

queso frito
fried cheese

Cut all the rind off the Manchego cheese and cut the cheese into ½-inch wedges.

Put the flour on a small plate and, working in batches of 6, dip each wedge in the flour, then in the beaten egg, then in the bread crumbs.

Heat half the olive oil in a nonstick skillet over medium heat, then fry the wedges in batches until golden—about 45 seconds each side. Drain on paper towels.

Wipe out the pan (to get rid of burnt bread crumbs) and fry the remaining batches in the same way.

Sprinkle with a pinch of paprika, if liked, and serve with quince paste and olives, if using.

*Note Membrillo is a thick paste made from quinces, a golden fruit related to the apple and pear, available in fall. Quinces are cooked into desserts, jellies, or jams, and into this sweetly smoky paste. Membrillo is also served with a good Manchego cheese instead of dessert in Spain.

8–10 oz. semi-cured Manchego cheese, 3 months old

2 tablespoons all-purpose flour

1 egg, beaten

2 cups lightly dried fine fresh white bread crumbs

⅔ cup olive oil

a pinch of oak-smoked sweet Spanish paprika (page 23)

to serve

membrillo (quince paste; optional)*

mixed olives, (optional)

serves 6

alioli

4–6 garlic cloves, crushed

1 whole egg

1 egg yolk

1 teaspoon freshly squeezed lemon juice

2 cups extra virgin olive oil

sea salt and freshly ground black pepper

serves 4

Put the garlic, egg, and egg yolk and lemon juice in a food processor. Blend until pale yellow. Keep the motor running and slowly pour in the olive oil, a little at a time. Blend well, until thick and silky, then add salt and pepper to taste. Serve at room temperature with fish or meat.

Alioli with potatoes

Put 1 lb. unpeeled new potatoes in a saucepan, cover with cold water, add a pinch of salt, and boil until tender. Drain and let cool. Slip off the skins, cut the potatoes into bite-size pieces, then serve with alioli as a dip.

aceitunas en escabeche
marinated olives

Put the olives in a bowl. Mix in the garlic, chiles, pepper, lemon, parsley, bay leaves, and salt, then transfer to a jar into which they just fit. Pour over the vinegar and the reserved brine. Shake well and let marinate at room temperature for 2 weeks.

Variation To marinate green olives, add 2 extra garlic cloves to the marinade and replace the chiles and other ingredients with 1 tablespoon crushed coriander seeds, 1 tablespoon crushed fennel seeds, 6 thyme sprigs, 4 rosemary sprigs, and the zest and juice of 1 orange. Cover with olive oil and marinate for 6 days.

1 lb. black Spanish olives, drained with brine reserved

4 garlic cloves, sliced

2 dried red chiles

8 black peppercorns

1 slice of lemon

4 sprigs of parsley

4 fresh bay leaves

a pinch of salt

1¼ cups red wine vinegar

almendras saladas
salted almonds

Pour 1 inch depth of olive oil into a saucepan and heat to 380°F. Test with a sugar thermometer, or drop in a small cube of bread— it should turn golden in about 30 seconds.

Fry the almonds until lightly golden. Drain, sprinkle with the salt and paprika, and mix well. Let cool slightly before serving.

2 cups blanched almonds

1 teaspoon coarse sea salt, finely ground

½ teaspoon oak-smoked sweet Spanish paprika (page 23)

olive oil, for frying

index

picture credits

Martin Brigdale
Pages 1, 6, 11, 14, 19, 28, 30, 35, 39, 44, 47, 56

Peter Cassidy
Pages 5, 8, 12, 17, 20, 22, 25, 27, 33, 36, 41, 42, 49, 50, 52, 55, 59, 60

David Munns
Page 2

Ian Wallace
Page 3

Noel Murphy
Endpapers

recipe credits

Julz Beresford
Pages 9, 13, 16, 21, 23, 24, 26, 32, 37, 38, 40, 43, 48, 51, 53, 54, 58, 61

Clare Ferguson
Pages 15, 18, 29, 31, 45, 46

Linda Tubby
Pages 10, 34, 57

conversion charts

Weights and measures have been rounded up or down slightly to make measuring easier.

Oven temperatures:

110°C	(225°F)	Gas ¼
120°C	(250°F)	Gas ½
140°C	(275°F)	Gas 1
150°C	(300°F)	Gas 2
160°C	(325°F)	Gas 3
180°C	(350°F)	Gas 4
190°C	(375°F)	Gas 5
200°C	(400°F)	Gas 6
220°C	(425°F)	Gas 7
230°C	(450°F)	Gas 8
240°C	(475°F)	Gas 9

Volume equivalents:

American	Metric	Imperial
1 teaspoon	5 ml	
1 tablespoon	15 ml	
¼ cup	60 ml	2 fl.oz.
⅓ cup	75 ml	2½ fl.oz.
½ cup	125 ml	4 fl.oz.
⅔ cup	150 ml	5 fl.oz. (¼ pint)
¾ cup	175 ml	6 fl.oz.
1 cup	250 ml	8 fl.oz.

Weight equivalents:

Imperial	Metric
1 oz.	25 g
2 oz.	50 g
3 oz.	75 g
4 oz.	125 g
5 oz.	150 g
6 oz.	175 g
7 oz.	200 g
8 oz. (½ lb.)	250 g
9 oz.	275 g
10 oz.	300 g
11 oz.	325 g
12 oz.	375 g
13 oz.	400 g
14 oz.	425 g
15 oz.	475 g
16 oz. (1 lb.)	500 g
2 lb.	1 kg

Measurements:

Inches	cm
¼ inch	5 mm
½ inch	1 cm
¾ inch	1.5 cm
1 inch	2.5 cm
2 inches	5 cm
3 inches	7 cm
4 inches	10 cm
5 inches	12 cm
6 inches	15 cm
7 inches	18 cm
8 inches	20 cm
9 inches	23 cm
10 inches	25 cm
11 inches	28 cm
12 inches	30 cm